# Thoughts in the Key of Yesterday

Leslie Watley

Credit/Source:

Steal Away to Jesus: Folk Songs of the American Negro (No. 1), 1907

Wade in the Water: a Negro spiritual first published in New Jubilee Songs as Sung by the Fisk Jubilee Singers (1901) by John Wesley Work II and his brother, Frederick J. Work

All Lives Matter: Source Unknown



ISBN: 978-0-692-46019-1

# DEDICATION

Thank you, God. Without you God, I am nothing, and I can do nothing. Thank you, God for gifting me with the ability to express myself through words.

This book is dedicated to my Mama and Aunt. Mama, thank you for establishing my foundation and giving me every opportunity to explore all the gifts God has blessed me with. Aunt Mary, thank you for giving me the courage to be me unapologetically. Your unwavering love and support has blossomed me into the woman I am today. I can never repay you for your love and support.

# CONTENTS

Acknowledgements i

**Thoughts**

Words Light 8
His Choice 9
A Prayer to God 11
Had You Known 12
But If 14
Sensitive 15
Frontage 16
Green with Envy 18
Perspective 20
Saying goodbye… A note to Christine 21
The Meeting 23
Privilege 26
America's Dream 28

**Feels**

One feeling 31
Another Feeling 32
Back to You 33
Heat 34
If Only You Knew 35
Mesmerized 36
You 37
Fool for You 38
*One More Feeling* 39
Numb 40
Awkward Space 41
Stolen Love 43
Default 44
Hurtful Words 45
Frozen Cold to Love 46
Fall for You 48
While I Wait 49
And for You I Wait 50
I Don't Know/Now You Know 52

# ACKNOWLEDGMENTS

Denise and Gekia, thank you for encouraging me to go public with my poetry. Without your persistence these poems would still be scattered around in different notebooks. Ever so thankful for my family and friends for consistently giving me encouragement and support throughout the process of writing this book. Special thanks to Tammy, Sika, Akiya, Aquil, April, Starr, Zac, Maria, and Michael.

To my amazing editor Melanie Figg and co-editor Sanco Singleton, thank you, thank you, thank you, I couldn't have done this without the both of you.

# Thoughts

## *Words Light*

Plug her in
To turn you on
Don't hesitate to take your turn
Give these words a chance to burn
A lesson that you'll love to learn

Yearning for this knowledge, while embracing this verbiage
Turning your world around to give new perspectives

## *His Choice*

Life for him hasn't always been easy
The cards that he was dealt
Required him to grow up much quicker than the average child
He received many wounds as gifts from hurt people
Abandonment, rejection, physical and mental abuse, and rape
These wounds would have destroyed most children
But he choose to live his life not dwelling on the hard times
The hard times made him, who he is today
While at times he questions why all these bad things happened to him
He realized that without those painful wounds
He may not have the perspective that he has now
He chooses to be happy no matter what
He draws from those hard times to respect the many good times

-Continued on page 10-

If only others could see that making this
choice can free you
Refuse to be a victim
Refuse to allow the past to consume you
You are in charge of your now and your
future
Life isn't always going to be easy
But chose to accept the challenge
Like bring it on!!!
Take on new perspectives
Accept the challenge
Live this life one step at a time
Free yourself, it is your choice

## *A Prayer to God*

Who am I?
Am I who you say I am?
You created me in the image of You
But what does that mean?
Am I great because I am a reflection of You?
What if I can't be what You say I am?
Looking deep within to try to see all that You say I am
Reflecting on my reflection that isn't always of You

Because of my sinful ways
Darkness invades
Leaving me unidentifiable

When my reflection is unrecognizable
I need You to capture the darkness within my soul with Your glorious light
So that I may one day know

Who I am.

## *Had You Known*

Looking back trying to remember the 21 year old you…
You see a younger you that is petrified
You are afraid to make mistakes
You want to prove everyone wrong
You want to stand on your own
You don't really see your beauty
You don't appreciate your body
You don't know your worth

If only you could return to the age 21 knowing what you know now
You wouldn't strive to prove folk wrong
You would embrace your curves and see your beauty
You would take chances like you were living in your final days
You would focus on your happiness
Knowing that time can't be reversed
You can strive to live with these regrets in mind
Only to acknowledge

-Continued on page 13-

That life is too short to have regrets
You are beautiful
The things that you don't like that you can change you can change
The things that you can't change you can pray that God will help you to accept them

You should take more risks
You will love you now and always
Because you know now what you should have known then

## *But If*

One shouldn't dwell on the "ifs" in life... If the "if" was ever a possibility, then why wasn't it made a reality?

## *Sensitive*

He is the type of person that feels everything
deeply
He would rather feel the pain from a punch
than the stab from a hurtful word
He even feels the words that are never spoken
that are translated from actions
He used to hate being so sensitive
Until he experienced the burn from a
coldhearted girl who broke his heart
Now he is grateful that he feels everything
He'd rather feel everything than to feel
nothing like her
Because it reminds him that he is alive

## ***Frontage***

*Chatter from them over there:*

*Oh so u kno, her car got repo da otha day. Chile say it ain't so… I was wondering why ole girl was getting off the number 5 wit dat fake ass MK. Err since that football playa broke up wit her…she stay frontin… we kno u ain't got it boo… but we see you boo.*

*Chatter from them over there:*

*He kno damn well that's his baby…Girl, he needs to get a job and support that baby… 30 years old and still livin at home wit his mama. But he got dem new J's though, he stay frontin.*

Why is she so afraid to be real?
Putting on this facade of what she thinks is acceptable behavior

-Continued on page 17-

Why is she afraid of being the one the ONE
called her to be?
Walking around giving off an aroma that
could never be traced back to her because she
can never duplicate a lie

See the phony that he represents is
inconsistent and unstable
Causing him great grief, which eventually
causes him to grieve himself because in the
midst of the lies he spread while being fake he
lost the essence of who he is, was and could
have been

Wake up my dear!

Breathe in this fresh new reality that begins
everyday
Explore the opportunity of you being you

Searching for you
Making mistakes and learning from them
Looking back only to remember where you
came from and why you must not return to
the fakeness that you once dwelled in

## *Green with Envy*

Green
That Mean Green
What did green ever do to you?
Green has so many connotations, too many to be fair
Did anybody ever stop and ask Green what it wanted?
No!?!? We just labeled it and defined its being without cause
Why can't things just be? Do titles really matter?
Are the leaves on this tree, here, outside of my window really green?
It's summer time and the tree is healthy and beautiful
Why can't the leaves be gold or purple or blue?
Why does envy have to be green?
What about yellow envy? The type of envy that can exist among friends
See yellow is a color that stands for friendship
So it makes perfectly good sense to be yellow with envy

-Continued on page 19-

Wishing that you had what your friends have
And what about Red?
Red is such a powerful color
Because it's meaning is ever-changing
Red… Passion and Desire
Red… Love
Red… Rage and Anger
Can't you have red envy? Why not? To be secretly envious of someone else's love.
Black Envy? That's a good one! The type of envy that causes death
You know that haters syndrome, so bad that it kills
Oh and don't forget White with envy…
I could hit so many angles with this one
I mean, when you are so envious of others that you pick them apart piece by piece so that you can steal the essence of what makes them, only to then to call it your own…
White with envy MAY just be the worst of them all!
I'm just saying, green needs a break…
Signed: Green with Envy

## *Perspective*

Everything looks so different, when the weather changes.

## *Saying goodbye… A note to Christine*

Christine, my only memories of you were given to me by the ones who stayed. The stories about you tormented my little heart. Your story was no fairytale. You left me …mom… at the fragile age of two.

When I thought about you, I felt numb. Because all those years I suppressed the need to express or articulate my feelings for you. Particularly due to the fact that I thought I would hurt the one who stood in the place that you chose not too.

I couldn't tell her how much I thought of you, needed you. To ask you why, to beg you to change your mind, to yell at you, and tell you that if you didn't need me… then…

How could I expose the weakness that you inflicted upon me?
Not that you knew, but you handicapped me, when you left.

-Continued on page 22-

Unwilling to be a victim, not wanting to be a hero…
I surged on… Choosing to forget you. But like with many things in my life, I failed.

Sometimes I have a hard time reconciling the pain that you caused.
Your decision will always impact my life.

But how it will impact my life is my decision.
And no matter how much it hurts…. I choose to see the positive.

Your choice could have crippled me, but it deepened me.
To be able to feel sympathy for others who are in similar situations.

But more importantly it has made me realize the importance of knowing,
Knowing what I have… so I'll never leave it.

## *The Meeting*

This tree on my back was the loan that afforded you your freedom.

This tree on my back is simply a constant reminder of a time so not far gone. This tree on my back roots extend to the very soul of each of you.
This tree on my back was a gift from a white man who considered himself my master.

But little did he know, I had no earthly master.

My heavenly master would never beat me down, for trying to stand on my own two feet.

The slaver thought when he beat me he owned me. But little did he know that with each lash of that whip he made me more determined to follow my true master.

*My Lord, He calls me… He calls me by the thunder….*

-Continued on page 24-

He thought the sting of that whip would keep me from stealing away.
It did the opposite. It made me want freedom more. It made me listen to my God as he beckoned for me, to….

*Wade in the water, Wade in the water, children.*
*Wade in the water. God's gonna trouble the water.*

You see this tree that is engraved on my back, was price that I paid for you to have a CHOICE.

Don't you get it!!! Your freedom's payment is on my back for life. Your ticket to this freedom is in your mind. And once that decision is made, there is no going back. When your mind has been freed you can only continue to run after the freer for more truths.

My brothers and sisters, this is just a meeting to steal away from our oppressors.

-Continued on page 25-

Don't be frightened if you realize some of our oppressors share our same skin color and don't be ashamed and hold your head down when you realize that you have oppressed yourself.

This meeting was called for all of you who haven't forgotten about the roots that extend from the grave that penetrate the actual essence of who we are.

And it serves as a reminder to the ones of you who have forgotten or claim to have never known about the great sacrifices that were made for each of you to walk freely…

But ask yourself… are you really free?

Don't let the message of these roots on my back that were planted by the water of my soul, that was carried from generation to generation by a seed wither and die because you choose not to make a choice to let the seed within you purpose.

## *Privilege*

This thing is given freely at birth
Not everyone will get it…
Some that have it don't feel that they have
it…
Regardless of the lack of the
acknowledgement of its existence
It is there
Some wonder what it would be like to have it
While others deny it
Only a few can describe it
Those without it say they have to…
Work harder
Be smarter
Love harder
Fight fair
Look safe
Be silent
Look innocent
Be like them
Accept second best
Get used to it
Be over looked
They are…

-Continued on page 27-

Criminalized
Devalued
Stereotyped
Boxed in
Treated unfairly
Outcaste by the color of their skin

## *America's Dream*

America, America what is your dream?

Is your dream that this land be a place where people of all nationalities can live together, while becoming better and having an opportunity to be anything that they want to be?

What happens when your dream, America, contradicts reality?

Was America's dream only meant for the privileged?

America, while I still love you, I am discouraged and heartbroken by the overwhelming amount of hatred that runs through your veins. Not everyone believes in your dream.

-Continued on page 29-

Hate group's actions buck at your dream, while spewing out venom that infects the weak-minded individuals that follow in hatred's footsteps.

Hatred in a land full of unspoken promises unraveling metaphorically, separating this nation by race, sex, economic status, sexual orientation, religion and so much more.

There's a problem in this country, and it must be acknowledged that not everyone believes that all lives matters.

I don't want to be a martyr.
I want to live.
Don't make me a victim, just so you can believe.

Oh America, if only the tears you shed could erase the hatred from this land. So that your dream, America, could manifest; everyone living together, harmoniously.

If that's your actual dream.

# Feels

Feelings rarely stay consistent… and can be compared to the weather… so don't get caught up in yesterday's windstorm… because it's simply an expression from a feeling that passed.

In the middle of the night when all the souls are resting… I wait for you, in my secret room.

## *Back to You*

Emotions have me locked up in a vicious
cycle that always brings me back to you
You've hurt me so bad and you cut me so
deep
That I gotta let go of you
But I don't know how
Cause baby I'm emotionally connected to you
Never would have thought that a girl like me
could fall for a boy like you

So I am trippin…
So I am trippin…
Over a guy like you…

I'm addicted to you in the worst way
I got this itch that that reminds me that I need
a refill of you
But I gotta let go of you
Cause baby I'm physically addicted to you
Never would have thought that a girl like me
would fall for a boy like you

## *Heat*

I want you…
Damn it I said I want you…
What's a girl gotta do,
To get a moment with you?

Let me entice you with the movement of my
Body, soul and mind

The way it sways left to right and up and
down

You better stay focused cause this rhythm that
I'm giving
Has been known to cause motion sickness

## *If Only You Knew*

The magic that I feel when I am with you
Sends sparks through my body
That ignites a fire through me…
The heat is so unbearable at times
I try to escape
But this love compound
Has no windows or doors
I'm trapped by your essence
So much so
That I see you everywhere
I feel you, I breathe you.

## *Mesmerized*

Can't take my eyes off of you
For the fear that I might miss something that you do
Or say...

Don't wanna miss my opportunity to invest my vernacular into your ear space
In hopes that it will connect with your right hemisphere and linger around a bit until you
Feel it

There is something about you...
Can't put my finger on it as yet, but whatever it is…
I want more of it.

## *You*

You, with your black skin, chiseled chin, deep succulent dimples, eyes that pierce me every time you look at me. Came into my life not so long ago with a promise that was never told. Why do you have such an affect on me? Is it your fingers that eloquently frisk my spinal cord with your perfect imperfect melody? Or is it the existence of your possibility? More on my bad side than my good side. But I still can't seem to give up on what I thought I saw in you. Spoke lies to me. Oh how I thought it was okay to love you, but you showed me that if I did, it would be one sided. We both knew that our love would never work but we both wanted to hold on. Our definitions of each other were so wrong but we lied to each other just to get along. Why didn't you have the courage to let go? You knew that I didn't. So here we are, both hurting… well at least I know I am. Wanting it to be better and normal. But how can we have normal if "we" being together made normal not normal. Because we can only exist in what if…

## *Fool for You*

Maybe it's the way you look at me, that captivates me.
Something about your eyes that makes me weak.
Just one glance and I'm hooked, like a bait worm on a hook.
Having this thing that I have for you is so unhealthy.
It's silently suffocating me.
I try to fight it.

But every time I do, you loosen your grip and allow me to catch my breathe.
And then you catch me again with the snare of your mouth.
Constantly losing a battle that was never meant to be fought.

Why can't I escape you?
Why do I enjoy the intoxicating pain that you put me through?

Baby I'm a fool for you….
You had me at first glance.

Let me go
If you know
You can't give me what I need.

## *Numb*

Can't explain it, but I know it's there
Pulling at me to remind me of its presence
It's neither good or bad but it sure ain't
unworried
I'm not okay with not knowing exactly what
you are?
And why you are here?
And how long you plan to stay?
Introduce yourself! Tell me your name
How is it that you feel okay with knowing me
and I not you?
Just wondering because I want to be able to
answer honestly when they ask me…
How are you?

## *Awkward Space*

Treading in a space that I'm not comfortable in…
I'm not alone because you are with me…

But I feel alone, because we are here for different reasons
At times I think we are on the same page because I want it to be so…

Until you hit me with the fact that we don't belong together
And it sends me colliding down, head first into reality…

Embarrassed to say I went there alone again…

But I was for sure, this time, things would be different… it would all be good
So I go for it again, full speed ahead
Blindly…

-Continued on page 42-

We laugh, share old memories, talk about
your side and my side of what happened…
Argue a little…

Then we get silent…

And in that silence is where it's revealed…

The awkward space that exist between you
and me.

## *Stolen Love*

Did you ever love me? I mean truly love
me…
You know, like Heath Cliff loved Clair…
Like Martin loved Gina…
Or…
Never mind
That wasn't reality, but you played your part
That was a show
Just like your love
Except no one told me you were acting
Why didn't you fill me in?
You played me smoother than the notes in a
lullaby
So smooth that most of our love seems like a
somber sleep
Until I'm jolted awake from the nightmare
that
We are no longer together…
But you did that!!!
Need an Oscar for that!!!
A round of applause for that!!!
Voluntary or involuntary
Either way you're guilty as charged

## ***Default***

My default is to hurt you
Before you hurt me
I've known me longer
Me, I can trust
You are so wavering in your love and devotion
One day you love me and the next day you hate me
I gotta protect me
Until you show me that I can trust you
Trust you with my heart
I didn't mean to hurt you… *when I said you weren't the only one*
I was just protecting my heart from your trickery
You tricked me into believing that I was special
But your actions dismissed me
So I got even and introduced you to default
The mean girl that always has my back
She protects me from the pain you inflict

## *Hurtful Words*

Wishing that I could edit time like Photoshop
I would erase, the hurt, the pain, and sadness
That spilled out of my mouth when I forgot
me
The bruises and unhealed wounds that were
gifts from someone hurting

*I hate you*

Should have reminded me to be more
careful…

*I wish I never met you*

If only I had immunity to your hurt

*You make me sick*

I wouldn't try to retaliate

*F*** you*

Regret following immediately

*But….*

When I remember that I can't take it back

*Sorry.*

## *Frozen Cold To Love*

Love, is an action word.
So many people know nothing of the word
Who am I to expect the love I am unwilling to give myself?
Love, why are you so foreign to me?
I want you
I yearn for you
I'll take you however I can get you
A'ha…. I say
Maybe that's the problem
I don't truly want you, the real you, love
I am simply caught up in the fixation of what I think you are…. *Love is easy and breezy.*
And not truly who you are…. *Love is patient. Love is kind.*
I could blame Disney for showing me unrealistic visions of love…
*Sleeping Beauty*
Or maybe it's your fault ex…
For giving me a brief moment of your unexpected casual hints of love
Nah who am I kidding…

-Continued on page 47-

Love you've always been there
Lurking…
Knocking at the door of my heart
Beckoning for me to answer
But I couldn't and wouldn't open the door to let you pour out
Your warmth
A warmth that never goes cold
Because I was too wrapped up
In my wakened mind that is frozen cold to love

## *Fall for YOU*

It's crazy the way love makes us do things we wouldn't normally do
We neglect ourselves to be everything to everyone
And it often goes unnoticed
Why do we sacrifice for love when we are empty inside?
Don't try to deny the black hole that resides inside
That grows bigger and bigger
Deeper and wider
Because you forgot to love you first
Stop overextending yourself
Take some time for you
Spoil you
Cherish you
Love you
Nurture you
Pray for you
Fall for you
Fall in love with YOU.

## *While I Wait*

While I wait on you, my beloved
I vow to not wait on the existence of who I
am to manifest into the person God has called
me to be
I will take this time to focus on me
Becoming a better me one day at a time
Indulging in new possibilities that will shape
me
Creating new depths
Exploring all that I can

## *And for You I Wait*

Sitting here thinking that I can never live without you
The oddity in this stream of thoughts is that I haven't met you yet
Before you look at me crazy, let me explain what is so evident to my soul
See I've waited for you…
For what seems like a thousand years

Dreamed about you…
Tall dark and handsome

Imagined our conversations…
Baby, you're so funny… say it again

Prayed for you…
God, please help him to love my imperfections

Pictured what our kids would look like…
Our son has your dimples

-Continued on page 51-

You must be magnificent because God is
testing me
He wants me to appreciate you
By making sure that I am completely prepared
to accept just how much He loves
me Because He made you for me and me for
you.

I cannot wait to say
Forever mine

## *I Don't Know/Now You Know*

In this world, lost and confused
But focused to find out why he doesn't know why
Everything about this situation tells him that he has no reason to feel the way he does
He wasn't wrong… well not entirely
But why does he feel so sad? He wanted to know the truth
And now that he has it
He's empty
Trying to understand himself
He can't seem to see outside of himself
To see what you see in him
His friends say *"you deserve better"*
But what is better? How can he know what is *"better"* if he's never felt *"better"*?
Is he to wait his entire life for something he knows not?
Why can't he see what you see that he deserves?
And life dear sweet old life presents the exact opposite or equal to what he is supposed to run from…..Everyday

-Continued on page 53-

All he can say is to be careful what you ask for
He knows that he shouldn't feel this way but he does
Empty…
Craving for…
Yearning for…
What you say he deserves
He can't put it into words to explain…
But he is certain in this for sure… that he knows nothing but what he feels…. And his feelings are deeper than even he knows… he doesn't know…
Did you know that your inner hate for yourself manifests on the outside of your body?
In the way you treat others
In the way you treat yourself
How critical you are of everyone, including yourself
Imagine what love could do

-Continued on page 54-

You can really love others and you can really love yourself
You could be at peace
You yearn for that love
So that you can love yourself and someone else

# ABOUT THE AUTHOR

Leslie T. Watley was born and raised in a small town in South Carolina. She has a Bachelor of Arts Degree in Mass Communications, from Benedict College. She currently resides in Maryland.

Made in the USA
Charleston, SC
13 November 2015